HEALING PRINCIPLES

Michael Scanlan, T.O.R.

with
Dave and Neta Jackson

D1601286

SERVANT BOOKS
Ann Arbor, Michigan

Copyright © 1987 by Michael Scanlan, T.O.R.
All rights reserved.

Cover design by Charles Piccirilli

Printed in the United States of America
ISBN 0-89283-357-2

88 89 90 91 92   10 9 8 7 6 5 4 3 2

HEALING
PRINCIPLES

This is not an introductory book on healing. I'm presuming some things. I'm presuming that you believe in healing and that you know how to pray generally for healing. I'm presuming that you've seen people healed and that I don't have to convince you that you should pray or that people do get healed when you pray.

What I want to do is step back and look at the past fifteen years during which the healing ministry in the Roman Catholic church has come alive, primarily in the context of the Catholic Charismatic Renewal. I want to consider: What works? What brings life? What has been most important?

I can only speak out of my experience in the healing ministry, but I want to share what I see are the ten key principles that have come alive for me and have stood the test of time.

Founded on the Rock

There's a basic Scripture that encourages us to approach life with our eyes open, identifying what's really solid rather than building on the sand of wishful thinking. It is what Jesus said in Luke 6:47-49:

> Any man who desires to come to me will hear my words and put them into practice. I will show you with whom he is to be compared. He may be likened to the man who, in building a house, dug deeply and laid the foundation on a rock. When the floods came the torrent rushed in on that house, but failed to shake it because of its solid foundation. On the other

hand, anyone who has heard my words but not put them into practice is like the man who built his house on the ground without any foundation. When the torrent rushed in upon it, it immediately fell in and was completely destroyed.

Sometimes we will experience the torrents of difficult illness. Maybe there will be people with terminal illness right in our own family; maybe people with whom we have prayed time and time again will not experience healing. Maybe we'll encounter situations we don't believe should have happened, like a youngster terribly mutilated in an automobile accident. The question is, when we face these situations, have we built on rock? Have we built on God's Word? And do we have something to sustain us and help us sustain others as we seek God's healing? It's easy to build on the sand of wishful thinking, but you'd better have your understanding of healing founded on rock or you'll be washed away, and a lot of people could be hurt.

Ten Key Principles

Another way to look at this is the Gospel illustration that we are to be wise stewards. For every situation we are to pull out the best of the old and the new and put it together. We're to see the new things God is doing, and we are also to understand the old; we're to understand his Word that lasts forever.

So, here are the ten most important principles that I have learned in the last fifteen years.

1. God is way ahead of us. Back in 1969, while I was rector of St. Francis Major Seminary, Father Jim Ferry, Joe Breault, and others prayed over me to be baptized in the Holy Spirit. It was a magnificent event. Every time I think of it, it stirs my spirit. That night God enveloped me—Father, Son, and Holy Spirit. I experienced a new power, and when I read the Word of God, it seemed so personal that it was like reading my own diary—not that it was about me; it was for me! The words were leaping off the page. It was a momentous occasion in my life.

First Fruits

But Father Jim and Joe went back to New Jersey, and there I was knowing nothing about the Charismatic Renewal. I tried to search out the people who could teach me, but there were no priests in Pennsylvania at that time who were "known" to be baptized in the Spirit. The only place I could find to go and learn was the Full Gospel Business Men's meetings. So I went to one of them. Being a priest, I was just as much an oddity to them as they were to me, so they put me at the head table. After the dinner was over, they announced that I would pray with anybody for "anything they wanted."

Sure enough, I was ushered off into a side room, and people started to line up. One fellow came to me and said, "Do you have a healing ministry?"

I said, "No."

"Do you pray for healing?"

"No."

"Well, would you at least pray with me?"

All I could say was, "Okay, as long as you don't count on anything happening." I couldn't figure it out; why me?

But then he said, "God told me to come to you for healing. You see, I'm legally deaf, and I've just lost my job. But I believe God is going to heal me, and so when he said, 'Go and ask that priest to pray with you,' I just came."

What could I do but pray?

I had no idea how to begin. I hadn't even watched anyone pray for healing before. So I bent over and put my fingers in each of his ears. There we were nose to nose and eye to eye, with me getting a crook in my back. All I could think of to say was: "God, please heal him." I think I just kept repeating it, when suddenly something like electricity started going through my two fingers.

My eyes got bigger. The "electricity" went into him, and his eyes got bigger. Finally, I said to myself, "As long as the electricity is going, I'd better keep the connection." That's all I knew, so I stayed there in that stance, even though I ran out of things to pray for, until eventually the "electricity" subsided. Then I quickly stood up and said, "God bless you," and quickly moved away.

I figured if it was a healing power going through me, I was into something really big, and I didn't have any room in my life for something really big at that point. If it wasn't healing, I didn't want to find out what it was. So I left. I didn't see him; I didn't ask him his name or anything.

Confirmation

A couple of months later I was driving through Pittsburgh when I sensed the Lord tell me, "Go to the prayer meeting," at a particular monastery I knew of. I was late and I wasn't going to be able to stay long, but I turned off the highway and went anyway.

I walked into the meeting and took a seat two rows from the back. Just as I sat down, a man, who couldn't have seen me come in, stood up about eight rows in front of me and said, "I have a witness to give. I've never been here before, but I want to tell you a story. Two months ago I was at a Full Gospel Business Men's meeting, and I asked a priest to pray for healing for me. He didn't want to do it. But I made him do it, and God totally healed me that night, and the doctor says I have a new eardrum.

"I've been going around seeking out Catholics because my whole life I've spread slander and lies about priests, sisters, and the Catholic church. I've repented, and I want to build church unity. I want to build us into one body. So I've come here tonight to ask your forgiveness."

You can picture what happened to me there, sitting in the back row. I said, "Wow, God is really up to something. God is way, way ahead of me. His plans and his designs are so much bigger than my thoughts."

That one principle has helped me more than anything else in the Charismatic Renewal: *God is way ahead of us.* If you hold on to that, you'll never create your own little ministry, your own special interest, or your own demands for how things should operate, but you'll always be seeking God and his plan.

God Alone Heals

Many of the foremost ministries we have known in Christianity have been based on the prophetic word. People hear what God is doing and announce it. Kathryn Kuhlman was a great healing minister in the Pittsburgh area. She had healing services every week. I went to a number of them. But she said that she never healed anyone. "All I do is listen to what God tells me he has already done, and then I ask the person who got healed that way to come up." It's true that she would then pray for the completion and the fullness of it, but she considered herself to be praying for those who had already been healed. Interesting, isn't it?

She was known as a great healer, and yet her ministry was based on the belief that God had already done it, and we just had to catch up. Pastor John Wimber gives a similar teaching, but he emphasizes that we can also see manifestations of God's healing power and then follow the signs with ministry.

Follow His Leading

I remember walking through a hotel lobby in Grand Rapids, Michigan, and seeing a big disturbance. A child was crying out, screaming, rolling around. There were a lot of people there trying to help that child and deal with the situation. I remember suddenly having that sense from God: "Go, and pray healing." This was in the middle of the big lobby of a hotel, but I went over, really convinced that God was telling me to do it. So, I asked the people if I could pray with their son, who had Down's syndrome. I prayed.

It was so clear that God had already started and wanted to reverse the illness in that boy. Since then, I have received many letters over the years from those parents. Every few years they write and tell me how well their son is doing in school and what a normal child he is.

The key is to hear God when he calls us and then to do what he calls us to do. In the FIRE ministry, I frequently call out words of knowledge on healing. Recently in Trinidad I announced a general healing of deafness. Twelve people came out of the stands, walked to the stage, and demonstrated complete healings in one or both ears. God is way ahead of us.

The Visitation of God

2. We are caught up in a visitation of the Lord. When I was in seminary, I used to read about the lives of saints and study what we call mystical theology. I always hoped to be present somewhere when something miraculous would happen. I used to think that God would do the miraculous only for really holy men and women. But now we see miracles happening all around us.

I have stood next to a woman who was blind, who couldn't see at all, when suddenly her sight was restored. I have been within a few feet of people who were deaf and had hearing aids, but who still couldn't hear well even with them, when

suddenly their hearing was restored.
I have watched the cripples throw
away crutches and canes. I've seen
the sick get out of their beds in the
hospital. These are great, great
things that have happened. How
should we understand them?

The disciples of John the Baptist
came to Jesus and asked, "'Are you
"He who is to come" or do we look
for another?' In reply, Jesus said to
them: 'Go back and report to John
what you hear and see: the blind
recover their sight, cripples walk,
lepers are cured, the deaf hear, dead
men are raised to life, and the poor
have the good news preached to
them'" (Mt 11:3-5). We've seen much
the same thing, and I believe that
our response ought to be the same
response as the disciples of John. We
ought to say, "We have found him.
We have found the Lord, and he lives
among his people, and he walks, and
he heals, and he restores life." I
believe we are experiencing a visitation of God.

What Is Our Response?

I want to give you a sense of the importance of the visitation of God. In Luke 19:36-46 we find three stages in the visitation of God. It was the Palm Sunday procession. Jesus was coming down from Bethany into Jerusalem, and the people were laying out the palms. Luke writes:

They spread their cloaks on the roadway as he moved along; and on his approach to the descent from Mount Olivet, the entire crowd of disciples began to rejoice and praise God loudly for the display of power they had seen, saying: "Blessed is he who comes as king / in the name of the Lord! / Peace in heaven / and glory in the highest!"
Some of the Pharisees in the crowd said to him, "Teacher, rebuke your disciples." He replied, "If they were to keep silence, I tell you the very stones would cry out." (Lk 19:36-40)

1. The first stage is the signs and wonders, the miracles.

2. The second stage is the people's response. Here, many responded appropriately by praising God. However, if God's people don't respond and say, "I see it. It's God. He's working," then the very stones can cry out because all creation is subject to him.

3. The third stage is the sad consequence of a failure to recognize God. We find it described as Luke continues:

> Coming within sight of the city, he wept over it and said: "If only you had known the path to peace this day; but you have completely lost it from view! Days will come upon you when your enemies encircle you with a rampart, hem you in, and press you hard from every side. They will wipe you out, you and your children within your walls, and leave not a stone on a stone within you, because you failed to recognize the time of your visitation."

Then he entered the temple and began ejecting the traders saying: "Scripture has it, 'My house is meant for a house of prayer' but you have made it a 'den of thieves.'" (Lk 19:41-46)

Because Jerusalem failed to be humble enough, open enough, and meek enough to recognize the wonders of God and to throw off people's notions of what the Messiah had to be like and what he had to do, Jesus said that the city would be destroyed. And we know that in 70 A.D., on Pentecost, the Roman army came in and leveled that city, and not a stone was left on a stone. The Romans erected crosses all around the city; the men were crucified, and the women and children were burned on the roofs. Jesus said it was because they did not recognize the time of visitation.

God's Purpose

It is very clear to me that a visitation of God starts with signs, wonders, healing, resurrections; moves to recognizing Jesus Christ as Lord, as Messiah, as the established Son of God to whom all lives should be submitted; and ends with judgment on those who didn't recognize it. God's house needs to be purified. I believe that as we get seriously into the healing ministry, we have to see that God's purposes are more than just the wonders. He wants a people submitted and committed to him. He wants a people of holiness who can reign with him in glory forever. As important as the healings are, the most important thing is that we are at the right hand of the Father with Jesus singing praises to God for all eternity.

The Gift of Faith

3. The gift of faith should be evident. God can always do what he wants, but time and time again Jesus said, "Your faith has made you whole." Faith is a key element. It is also a gift. It is not more strenuous will power. It is not gritting your teeth.

And it is not wishful thinking. "Faith is confident assurance concerning what we hope for, and conviction about things we do not see," as the writer of Hebrews called it (11:1). And that is a gift. You don't get that total conviction and certainty except by the grace of God. We've got to pray for it. We've got to use what God gives us and build on it in our healing ministries.

Whose Faith?

I've noticed, both in the Scriptures and in practice, that the faith may be in different people. For instance:

1. *The faith may be that of the recipient.* The greatest example of this is Mark 5 and Matthew 9 where the woman touches the hem of Jesus' garment. Jesus didn't even know it was happening until the power went out, and then he told her it was her *faith* that healed her—it was not his garment, not even Jesus' initiative.

2. *Faith may be in the minister.* In

Mark 3, it is very interesting that Jesus healed a man with a withered hand when there is no indication that the man had any particular faith. He just had a withered hand, and Jesus decided to heal him. The faith was in the minister of healing.

3. *Faith may be on behalf of another.* Two very fascinating passages are in Matthew 9 and Mark 2. Both passages explicitly say that Jesus responded to the faith of those who brought the paralytic. So it seems that the faith of others can play a great part in healing.

Pray for Faith

But what I find overall is that we should seek and *expect* a special gift of faith. If we don't have it, we ought to pray for it. I would suggest that one of the most prudent things you can do before praying for healing is to pray for faith. Pray for what we call a "charismatic faith," which is a faith that is infused with certainty and confidence.

One experience I had concerning the role of faith so greatly impacted me that I have used it as a teaching example many times. It occurred many years ago after I baptized my niece. I stopped by my brother's home a few months later to see how things were going. Everyone was quiet until someone finally said, "Mike, Darlene is deaf. She can't hear at all. We've taken her to a couple of doctors. We've taken her to Columbia Medical Center. She's been tested in every way, and she'll never hear."

I sat down and thought of that little baby and of the whole family. As I sat there, I was just overcome with God's love for that girl. I remember being certain that God was going to move in that situation. So I said, "May I go to her?" I went in and anointed her with oil. When I came out, I said to my brother, "God moved. Something happened."

It was a week later that my brother was leaving her room and slammed the door, and she cried. He thought about it and realized that that wasn't supposed to happen. So he went back and slammed it again. She cried. He stood there slamming the door—wham, wham, wham. Each time she would cry out the instant she heard the door. They took her for new tests and found that she had better than normal hearing and is doing very well today.

I experienced God giving me that faith, that certainty, that confidence I needed so that I could act. My experience at the Full Gospel Business Men's meeting is a very clear example of the minister not having the faith. The deaf man had the faith, and I didn't. But in both instances the faith was a gift from God.

We hear a lot about "claiming" healings. If God has told you something, and you are sure it was God, then stand on it and claim it. But if he hasn't, then you'd better find out what he has in mind before you claim anything.

The Ministry of Healing

4. There are special ministries of healing. There are specific gifts for specific purposes, and they are given to specific individuals. God has decided that some are going to have a healing ministry and some aren't. He has also decided in his own way—I don't know why or how much it has to do with education, background, or personality—that these ministries are going to work differently. And they do.

Years ago I was with Sister Briege McKenna. Briege was supposed to give a seminar on healing, but she arrived a few minutes late and stood up and said, "God loves us, and he heals. I don't think I have anything more to say. Suppose we just pray for healing." She went down and she started to touch people, and they started to get healed. She has a powerful one-on-one ministry, and many have been healed of terminal diseases through her prayers. But that's her style.

Father Ed McDonough has his own approach which God anoints. He has a "holy hour." He may recite something from a book; he may read litanies in Latin; he may do whatever he is inspired to do at the time. You may think the healing service is never going to start. I've seen people yawn and get restless, and a few have even started to leave. But when the hour is up, he just says, "Well now, Lord, show us the signs and wonders." Then he says, "First we'll call up those who were blind who have gotten their sight back." The first time I was present, I didn't want to look. I was afraid that nothing would happen, but a fellow with dark glasses and a cane came down the aisle and said, "I can see." Then Father Ed called all those who had been deaf, and sure enough another group came forward, and then the crippled. He didn't pray for them until after they were healed. He just had his holy hour which God told him to make first.

Again, I don't advise you to make a

holy hour and just say, "Let the blind and the deaf come up." The point is: there are special ministries; there are things God does with certain people which we should reverence and respect.

I've known many Protestant brothers and sisters with specialized ministries in legs and backs. You may think that sounds funny, but God does things that way sometimes, and we are called to respect specific ministries. First Corinthians 12:9 says, "by the same Spirit another is given the gift of healing." That happens, and it happens according to God's way.

Healing Power for All

5. Ordinary healing power is available to all believers. James 5:16 says, "pray for one another, that you may find healing." That is addressed to all believers, and I don't believe Scripture would tell us to do that if God didn't intend to grant healing power as a result of that prayer.

Ordinary healing usually operates

in accordance with jurisdiction,
along the lines of your relationships.
When I see sick children, the first
thing I say is, "Father and mother,
pray. You've got the jurisdiction. God
has put you there. Stir up your faith.
Pray for the gift of faith and pray
that your child may be healed." I
believe that is the ordinary way God
wants those children healed.

I believe there is an ordinary
jurisdiction in pastors for their own
flock members. They ought to feel a
sense of authority, protection, and
power when they are ministering to
those under their care. In other
words, it is through God-ordered,
God-established relationships that
much ordinary healing happens.

There is one very good reason for
this: that is the way our love flows.
God heals us because he loves us.
And whom you love, you can best
pray for. But too often we are the
last ones to pray for those who are
closest to us. Too often we care so
much that we think we have to go
out and get an expert. No, *you* pray.
Say, "I love you; may I pray for you?"

And know that God will answer the prayer.

How will he answer it? I don't know; all I know is that he will answer. God is not going to resist a prayer uttered in faith and love, in a relationship he has established.

How Should We Pray?

There are three things that we ought to do:

1. We ought to persevere in our prayer. That's most important. Most people I know pray for about as long as it takes to swallow two aspirin. We'll give the doctor half of our day sitting in a waiting room, but we won't spend more than a couple of minutes praying. We need to be available, persevering until there is healing.

2. Pray with the laying on of hands. I first prayed this way because I saw it working. The laying on of hands is a real instrument of God's power to bring forth healing. It is significantly different than praying for someone from a distance, and it frequently accompanies the reports of healing in Scripture.

3. *Anoint with blessed oil.* Oil has been set aside in the church from the beginning as a sacramental sign to be used for healing. Again, James 5:14 says, "Is there anyone sick among you? He should ask for the presbyters of the church. They in turn are to pray over him, anointing him with oil in the Name [of the Lord]." My conviction about this was strengthened by a recent trip I took to Medjugorje, Yugoslavia. From all accounts, Mary has been appearing nightly to a group of children there for the last three years. They belong to a little prayer group in the St. James parish in Medjugorje. One night while appearing to them, they asked Mary, "How should we pray?" And she said three things: "Lay on hands, use oil, and persevere in your prayer."

Healing through the Sacraments

6. There is a special healing in each sacrament. The sacraments are the special encounters we have with Jesus where there is already a pledge from God that he will bless us through them.

In confession inner healings often occur. Going beyond confession to seek healing is important so that people don't have to confess the same things every week or every month.

In the anointing of the sick healing power is clearest. The priest has one or two prayers to choose. One asks primarily for a happy death. The other asks primarily for restoration and immediate healing. I've already noted James 5:14 about calling the presbyters and anointing with oil. The next verse continues, "This prayer uttered in faith will reclaim the one who is ill, and the Lord will restore him to health."

In the Eucharist we ought to see the risen body of the Lord Jesus Christ, the healthiest body there is. It brings health to us. So many times healings are confirmed and completed in the Eucharist. At Lourdes, of course, they carry the Eucharist in a procession of benediction, and the healings that happen then are the only ones that they record.

Confirmation is also a special time for healing. I've seen a strengthening for discipling and witnessing, a kind of inner healing there.

Baptism. At Steubenville we baptize by immersion, during the Eucharist. Most of the time parents testify to a decided change in the baby through the sacrament of baptism. We've seen rashes disappear immediately. We've seen many cases of compulsive crying disappear permanently. Note that we also have a whole congregation praying for healing.

Matrimony certainly heals many experiences of past rejection, sexual scars, and unwillingness to love and receive love. People really can be healed and transformed in that sacrament when there's real prayer and faith.

Ordination frequently brings a sense of being commissioned by God and gives authority to go forth. Many priests testify to a significant new strengthening of character which began at their ordination.

The Power of Intercession

7. Intercession is a powerful force for healing. When intercession is accompanied with fasts and vigils, it is especially powerful for healing. We are told to pray for one another that we may find healing. The children asked Mary at Medjugorje whether they should pray to her or to Jesus. She said, "Pray to Jesus; I can't do anything for you of myself. But if you ask me, I'll pray with and for you." Mary is established as an intercessor. Have Mary pray with you. Ask her. She wants your healing.

This year on the campus at Steubenville, about eighty people went through an evangelism program in the fall and then the Life in the Spirit Seminars. Then came the night to pray with them for the baptism in the Spirit. About one hundred people were caring for the eighty or so that were being prayed with. But two hundred other students showed up and interceded on their behalf for three and a half hours. That is the kind of intercession we ought to practice.

Fast and Pray

During Holy Week the students had heard that last year those of us in the Servants of Christ the King, the community that is connected with University Chapel, had gone on a three-day bread and water fast in response to the message from Medjugorje to fast for the conversion of the world and for peace. So the students came and said, "We want to fast, too. What can we do?" So I told them what we had done, and three hundred and sixty students out of a little over four hundred students that were on campus during Holy Week signed up for a three-day bread and water fast. The last night we went into the chapel and we interceded—not for the students but for their relatives, friends, and others. By the next day testimonies were already coming in of people being healed of cancer and internal diseases.

We should trust that God answers prayer. We've got to believe in intercession.

Break All Bondages

8. Bondages should first be broken. Bondages to sin and to evil spirits should first be broken before healing prayer is administered. It is such simple, practical advice. When you are getting resistance, when people aren't responding, when your prayer isn't having any effect, check for sin and the need to repent.

When Jesus healed the paralytic, the first thing Jesus said was, "Your sins are forgiven you."

Sometimes there are blocks that you come against in your ministry that feel like a force that won't move. At those times it is important to take authority in the name of Jesus and learn how to cast out the interference of evil spirits. Then the situation will be open, and healing can happen. Ephesians 6:12 says, "Our battle is not against human forces but against the principalities and powers, the rulers of this world of darkness, the evil spirits in regions above." We need to be reminded over and over again that when situations aren't responding, there may be alien forces creating a sense of darkness, a coldness. Dealing with those evil spirits is a part of a healing ministry.

Follow-Up Ministry

9. Sustain healing with whole-life pastoring. It's very important to follow up a healing. You shouldn't cut off contact after a person is healed. The same situations that brought on the problem in the first place will usually bring back the problem or the sickness if the root causes aren't cared for. There are three reasons why you need pastoral follow-up.

1. Many healings are lost because of the continuing circumstances that caused the sickness. Sometimes something is sexually related, and the person remains in a bad sexual relationship. Sometimes it's tension related, and nothing is done to relieve the tension. Sometimes the presence of evil spirits is not dealt with, and the person continues to be exposed to them. Sometimes a person continues to be exposed to temptations. Pay attention to pastoral follow-up, and then people won't lose their healings.

2. What's received in faith should be maintained in faith. In other words, you need to build up the faith of the people who have received healings. Over and over again we have seen people receive healings and then begin to doubt that it ever happened and wonder whether they imagined or dreamed it all. If they persist in that kind of doubt, it is likely that the healing will disappear. What is established in faith must be maintained in faith.

3. Growth in Christian character is essential. There are many inner healings that will not remain if you don't build up the character of the person. We shouldn't keep having to provide inner healing for a person. The character of the people in our congregations should be built up in virtue and in God. They ought to come to the point where they are the ones who are praying with others for inner healing. God's interested in permanent solutions.

When Jesus Returns

10. Not every Christian will be healed until Jesus returns. The healing ministry is limited by the conditions of our sinful world. There simply will be situations that don't respond with restored physical health despite perseverance in prayer. Basically, paradise won't occur until Jesus comes again to bring everything into fullness. It won't come before that. So there's always going to be a limitation in our ministries. There's always going to be a lack of the fullness of what you pray for.

It's for this reason that men like St. Paul struggled with sickness. It's for this reason that a man like Smith Wigglesworth, who was one of the most extraordinary healing ministers that we've had in Britain and the United States, actually passed hundreds of gall stones while ministering great healings to other people. Still, he himself was not healed. He was a sign of the church; he was a sign that there is still a time of suffering that won't be completed until Jesus comes again.

What Does This Mean?

It means that anything can be healed, but not everything will be healed. You've got to face the reality.

Why won't they be healed? There can be many reasons. Sometimes our sickness builds character. Sometimes we're called to a special mission of reparation. The way we evaluate such situations is to ask whether the fruit of the Spirit is evident. In other words, when God's in the situation and responding to our prayer, even though the physical disease might not be healed, we should see the evidence of God's work. We ought to see the peace beyond understanding that the world cannot give. We should see the love, joy, patience, endurance, kindness, generosity, faith, mildness, and chastity that are the fruit of the Spirit, the fruit of God's working that we read of in Galatians 5. When we see these things happening, then we should step back and say, "Could it be that this person is special, that in this case it is in God's plan that this person work through and with the disease?"

The Truest Healing

God always answers prayer. He doesn't always answer it the way you might prefer. Remember my first illustration about my experience with the deaf man? I didn't know anything about healing or God's plan to build church unity. I didn't know the great purposes of God, and you and I still don't know all the great purposes of God.

One time Father Ed McDonough said at his holy hour, "Sometimes we have the wrong idea about healing. For instance, the greatest healing of all would be if we got struck by lightning and everybody died." Everybody said, "What?" And he said, "Then we'd be in glory with the Lord, and isn't that the place where we really want to be?"

Other Books of Interest from Servant Books

Let the Fire Fall
Michael Scanlan, T.O.R.

Tells how the Holy Spirit revolutionized the life of Father Mike Scanlan. A bold proclamation of the catching force of the Holy Spirit in the world today, and a testimony to the spiritual truth that all members of the body of Christ can be faithful vessels of the transforming power of God. *$6.95*

Straight from the Heart
A Call to the New Generation
Fr. John Bertolucci

America's best-known Catholic evangelist speaks frankly about the tough questions that young people face today. Encouragement, advice, and solid wisdom to lead you into a deeper and more satisfying relationship with Jesus Christ. *$4.95*

Reflections on the Gospels
Daily Devotions for Radical Christian Living
John Michael Talbot

Approximately four months of daily meditations from the gospels that reveal much of what motivated John Michael Talbot to abandon all in order to follow Christ and live a simple life, marked by poverty, chastity, and obedience. *$5.95*

Available at your Christian bookstore or from
**Servant Publications • Dept. 209 • P.O. Box 7455
Ann Arbor, Michigan 48107**
Please include payment plus $.75 per book
for postage and handling
*Send for your FREE catalog of Christian
books, music, and cassettes.*